Anointed in the Spirit

in the Spirit

Sponsor
Booklet

A High School Confirmation Program

saint mary's press

The publishing team included Maura Thompson Hagarty, development editor; prepress and manufacturing coordinated by the production departments of Saint Mary's Press.

Printed in the United States of America

2823

ISBN 978-1-59982-109-2

Contents

Welcome!

You have been asked to walk with a candidate as she or he prepares to celebrate the Sacrament of Confirmation. By accepting that invitation, you will be able to help a young person grow in relationship with both Jesus and the Church. This is an honor and a privilege.

The Confirmation preparation process can be—almost certainly will be—a time of spiritual and religious renewal and transformation for both you and the candidate. When it's all over, you will likely echo the words of countless sponsors who have walked this journey before you: "I gained so much more than I ever gave to the candidate." You may even want to take the journey again with another young person.

Now pause for a moment and reflect on how those opening paragraphs struck you. What feelings and thoughts did they generate in you? Here are some possibilities:

- This sounds great!
- This is pretty intimidating stuff.
- My faith is the most important thing in my life. It will be exciting to help a young person discover that too.
- I'm not even sure about my own faith. How can I help lead a young person through all this religious stuff?

You may, in fact, be feeling and thinking all these things at once. Depending on your past experience, just about any thoughts and feelings are justified as you begin this process. This guide will provide you with enough background and direction to make your experience as a sponsor both enjoyable and meaningful.

About This Guide

This guide is designed to ensure that your experience as a sponsor is positive. Here is what you will find in this guide:

- information about the Sacrament of Confirmation and an overview of what will happen at the celebration of the sacrament
- a discussion about the role of the sponsor within the Confirmation process
- practical ideas for building a relationship with your candidate
- guidance for effective conversations with young people

- five guided conversations, with step-by-step instructions, on the topics of God, Jesus, the Holy Spirit, the Church, and faith
- an overview of central characteristics of Catholicism
- a collection of prayers

All this information is presented as briefly and as clearly as possible. If, after reading this guide, you find that you would like more information, please consult your parish's program coordinator.

A Closing Thought

The role of the sponsor is both a challenge and a privilege. Walking with a young person through the process of preparing for Confirmation can be a time of spiritual renewal for both of you. We are grateful that you have said yes to this invitation, and we trust that you will be too. Remember always that the Spirit of God walks with you!

Chapter I

The Sacrament of Confirmation and Anointed in the Spirit

The Sacrament of Confirmation

The candidate you are sponsoring is continuing on the path of Christian initiation by preparing to celebrate the Sacrament of Confirmation. Confirmation is one of the Church's three Sacraments of Initiation. The three—Baptism, the Eucharist, and Confirmation—are the foundation of the Christian life. Baptism is the first sacrament celebrated, because it makes us members of Christ and part of the Church. Confirmation strengthens us for the Christian life and completes baptismal grace. The Eucharist nourishes us with Christ's Body and Blood throughout our lives. It is the high point of Christian life. All the sacraments, including Confirmation, are oriented toward it.

When the candidates are confirmed, they will be anointed with Chrism, consecrated perfumed olive oil. The bishop will lay hands on them and anoint them on the forehead. He will say their name and then say, "Be sealed with the Gift of the Holy Spirit"(*The Order of Confirmation*, 27). This anointing will confirm the anointing they received at Baptism, and they will receive an outpouring of the Holy Spirit. This does not mean the Holy Spirit is not already present and active in their lives. The outpouring of the Holy Spirit at Confirmation makes the candidates more like Christ and gives them added strength to live as Christians. Their bond with Christ grows stronger and their connection to the Church becomes stronger.

Overview of Anointed in the Spirit

Anointed in the Spirit supports an approach to faith formation for Confirmation called liturgical catechesis. This involves a three-part process: (1) preparation for Confirmation, (2) celebration of Confirmation, and (3) reflection after the celebration of Confirmation. Ideally, you will have a role—encouraging and supporting your candidate—during all three parts of the process and beyond.

Preparation for Confirmation

The program offers eight sessions designed to prepare the candidates for the Sacrament of Confirmation. The Order of Confirmation is the point of departure for the sessions. This means the sessions focus on an aspect of the Confirmation liturgy. The candidate handbook has a chapter that corresponds to each of these sessions. (The program co-ordinator will be able to provide you with detailed information about how Anointed in the Spirit is being implemented in the parish, what the specific expectations of sponsors are, and what any additional program components such as a retreat, service work, sessions with sponsors, and meetings with parents may involve.)

The following overview is meant to give you a general idea about the preparation sessions that are part of Anointed in the Spirit.

Session 1: Being a Candidate

The first session relates to the presentation of the candidates (see *The Order of Confirmation,* 21). The session explores the idea of being a candidate and being presented to the bishop.

Session 2: Baptism: Waters of New Life

This session invites the participants to reflect on their own cele-bration of Baptism and to explore the significance of Baptism for their lives. Deepening one's understanding of the meaning of Baptism is a helpful way to prepare for Confirmation because of Confirmation's close relationship to Baptism.

Session 3: Renewing Baptismal Promises

This session prepares the candidates for the Renewal of Baptis-mal Promises that takes place during Confirmation (see *The Order of Confirmation,* 23). The Baptismal Promises are listed in appendix 8.

Session 4: The Laying on of Hands

This session explores the meaning and significance of the laying on of hands in the Order of Confirmation (see *The Order of Confirmation,* 24–25).

Session 5: The Gifts of the Holy Spirit

The focus of this session is the consecratory prayer in which the bishop asks the Father to send the Holy Spirit on the candidates and give them the Gifts of the Holy Spirit (see *The Order of Confirmation,* 25). These gifts are listed in appendix A.

Session 6: Being Anointed by the Holy Spirit

This session explores the anointing with Chrism, the central symbolic action in the Order of Confirmation (see *The Order of Confirmation,* 26), and the significance of the outpouring of the Holy Spirit at Confirmation.

Session 7: The Eucharist: The Heart of the Church's Life

This session explores the significance of celebrating Confirmation within the Mass, the usual practice unless there are special circumstances.

Session 8: Celebrating the Sacrament of Confirmation

This session involves a brief walk-through of the Order of Confirmation and leads the participants through a process for reflecting on the Word that will be proclaimed at Confirmation.

Celebration of Confirmation

The preparation period leads to the high point: the celebration of the Sacrament of Confirmation. At the celebration, you will accompany your candidate and present him or her to the bishop for the anointing. You will place your right hand on your candidate's shoulder at the time of the anointing and either you or your candidate will give your candidate's name to the bishop. After Confirmation you are encouraged to continue your special role and help your candidate live out his or her Baptismal Promises.

Reflection After Celebration of Confirmation

Sessions 9 and 10 are designed for use during the weeks following the celebration of Confirmation. This part of the process, called mystagogy, is reflection on the mystery. The purpose of the mystagogical sessions is to deepen the confirmands' understanding of the sacrament and lead them outward into mission.

Session 9: Mystagogy I: Reflecting on the Order of Confirmation

This session provides the participants with an opportunity for re-flection on Confirmation and a further exploration of its meaning and significance for their lives.

Session 10: Mystagogy II: Reflecting on God's Word

Session 10 provides a mystagogical reflection on one of the readings from the celebration of Confirmation. A session extension introduces the confirmands to *lectio divina* and encourages them to make prayerful reading of the Scriptures a regular part of their lives as fully initiated Catholics.

Chapter 2

The Role of the Confirmation Sponsor

The role of a person who sponsors a young adolescent Confirmation candidate roughly parallels the role of godparents who accompany a catechumen through the Rite of Christian Initiation of Adults (RCIA). The RCIA describes the godparents' role in this way:

> Godparents are persons chosen by the candidates on the basis of example, good qualities, and friendship, delegated by the local Christian community, and approved by the priest. It is the responsibility of godparents to show the candidates how to practice the Gospel in personal and social life, to sustain the candidates in moments of hesitancy and anxiety, to bear witness, and to guide the candidates' progress . . . They continue to be important during the time after reception of the sacraments when the neophytes [the newly initiated] need to be assisted so that they remain true to their baptismal promises. (11)

Today many dioceses and parishes base their expectations of Confirmation sponsors on this understanding of RCIA godparents. Consider the following description of the role, taken from the Confirmation guidelines of one diocese:

The sponsor is . . .
- a model of how a person of faith lives in today's world
- a friend or relative who knows the candidate and can witness to the maturing faith of the candidate before the community
- a guide, a confidant, and a listener
- a learner who is interested in personal growth as she or he walks the faith journey with the candidate
- one who will continue after Confirmation to walk the faith journey with the candidate and invite her or him into fuller participation in parish life and service

Some sponsors (again, you may be one of them) may well enter the preparation process thinking that their role will be largely ceremonial and not too demanding. Then they'll read a description of the role like the one cited and break into a cold sweat, questioning why they said yes and what they have gotten themselves into. Here we provide a response to those questions that alleviates such concerns and helps such sponsors relax and at the same time remains true to the directives of the Church and the ideal of the sponsor that the Church holds up for us.

So, What's the Point?

What if, when you were recruited by a candidate, you expected a largely ceremonial role, only to discover that your role is much more active and involved? How do you feel as you review guidelines for sponsors like those you just read? How can you look at the ideal characteristics of the sponsor and not feel inadequate, or worse, hypocritical? Following are a few observations that will help put these issues in perspective.

Look to Canon Law

First of all, be aware that the official Church policies regarding Confirmation sponsors are actually much narrower and far less intimidating than the ideals reflected in many diocesan guidelines. According to canon law, sponsors must have the following qualifications (based on canon 893, which in turn refers to canon 874, a description of the qualifications for baptismal sponsors):

- A sponsor must be at least sixteen years old, unless the diocesan bishop has established a different age requirement or the pastor has determined a need for an exception.
- A sponsor must be a fully initiated Catholic (one who has celebrated Baptism, Confirmation, and the Eucharist) who "leads a life of faith in keeping with the function to be taken on" (Code of Canon Law, canon 874).
- A sponsor must not be bound by any Church penalty.
- A sponsor must not be the parent of the one to be baptized (or, by extension, confirmed).

It should be noted that canon 893 expresses that it is desirable for Confirmation candidates to choose their baptismal godparent or sponsor as their Confirmation sponsor. This reflects an effort by the Church to stress the close link between Baptism and Confirmation.

See Yourself as a Companion on the Journey

Most of us live with such an inflated sense of what it means to be Christian that we find the notion of being a role model for young people not only intimidating but even a bit arrogant. We assume that a Christian is someone who has already arrived at spiritual perfection. Then we look in the mirror and see a person with glaring shortcomings and weaknesses—limited knowledge, maybe a bad temper, impatience with others, a lack of trust in the love of God. In fact, we're so weak and ill-equipped that we look as bad as . . . the Apostles!

Jesus didn't build his ministry around those with encyclopedic knowledge of Judaism or all sorts of public acclaim as leaders of the community; in fact, those were the very people who gave him fits! Why do we assume it is different now?

Rather than seeing yourself as a role model for your candidate, think of yourself as your candidate's companion on the journey of faith. You may have a little more experience than he or she does, but you share the same human and spiritual hungers, the same search for meaning, the same struggles with the human condition, the same hope for relief from all the hurts and hurdles of life. And of course, you have the same deep hope that in Jesus we can find our salvation from all the things that keep us from fullness of life.

Your candidate doesn't need you to be anyone other than who you are—one who cares deeply and takes the journey of faith seriously enough to want to walk it with him or her. Paradoxically, if you just relax and enjoy that shared journey, you may well become a role model for your candidate.

Keep It Simple

Think about your strongest, deepest relationships. How did they develop? What now sustains them? For most of us, relationships aren't built on the dramatic stuff of movies or on the high-energy events of TV sitcoms; rather, normal relationships evolve slowly over time, developing from brief and often simple connections and exchanges. A thoughtful comment, a funny aside, a simple meal, a casual walk together, a small gesture of care—these are the things on which good relationships are built.

The next two sections of this guide offer practical strategies for fostering your relationship with your candidate and provide step-by-step guidance for having significant conversations. With the direction provided by this guide, and with the support of the Confirmation coordinator, other sponsors, your candidate's parents, and the community of faith to which you belong, you already have what you need to be an effective sponsor. The key is not to create unrealistic or unreasonable expectations for your relationship with the candidate. Make a commitment to do what you can and not to stress over what you cannot do. Do what you can, and God will do what you can't!

Chapter 3

Practical Ideas for Building a Relationship with Your Candidate

In this chapter, you will find concrete, practical suggestions on how to build and sustain a solid relationship with your candidate, one that will support the goals of the preparation process and make the Order of Confirmation a meaningful celebration for both of you.

Let these ideas spark your imagination and creativity. Trust your intuition about what will work well with your candidate, particularly as you get to know each other better. Most of all, relax and enjoy the time together.

An Important Note

Appropriate and healthy relationship boundaries are real concerns any time adults interact with young people. In light of heightened public awareness of and attention to child protection issues, we must ensure that a safe and healthy relationship is maintained between the adults and the young people who spend time together. In fact, all dioceses have specific guidelines for adults who work with young people. Criminal background checks and references for those engaged in ministry are some of the tools that measure the quality of the adults working with young people. Check with the Confirmation program coordinator about diocesan requirements concerning criminal background checks and the use of volunteer covenants.

In ministry with young people, several practical guidelines to keep in mind include the following:

- Providing a young person with an alcoholic beverage, tobacco, or drugs is never allowed.
- Touching must be age-appropriate and based on the need of the young person and not on the need of the adult. Physical contact must be avoided when an adult is alone with a young person.

- Adults should not be alone with a young person in a residence, sleeping facility, locker room, restroom, dressing facility, or other closed room or isolated area that is inappropriate to a ministry relationship. Adults must always meet with young people in visible and accessible areas. One-on-one meetings with a young person are best held in public areas.
- It is always a safe practice to have two adults in the area where young people are present.
- Driving alone with a young person should be avoided.
- Engaging in physical discipline of a young person is unacceptable.
- Taking an overnight trip alone with a young person from the parish or school community who is not a member of your immediate family is prohibited.
- Topics, vocabulary, recordings, films, games, or the use of computer software or any other form of personal interaction or entertainment that could not be used comfortably in the presence of parents must not be used with young people. Sexually explicit or pornographic material is prohibited.
- If anyone (adult or minor) abuses a young person in your presence, take appropriate steps to immediately intervene and to provide a safe environment for the young person. Report the misconduct.
- Be proactive in identifying young people who may be vulnerable to, or at risk for, unhealthy relationships. Adults can have a positive influence on young people by sharing the message that they are important in God's eyes and that they are created with dignity. This can reduce the possibility of their falling into the traps of those who tell them love is just physical.

How to Relate

Engage in One-Minute Ministry

Ask yourself if there any simple, quick ways you can show interest in, affirm and support, or make a quick connection with your candidate. For example, if a significant school-related activity is coming up, you might want to make a quick call, jot down a note of support before the event (or offer congratulations or condolences after it), or send an e-mail. Be aware that for many young people, almost anything qualifies as significant—a test or class presentation, a tryout for a play, an athletic event, a date, and so on.

Try to make a habit of thinking this way—looking for quick and simple ways to connect with your candidate—almost one minute at a time. Such brief connections often help create and sustain great relationships. Also, attending to such little things relieves the burden of having to arrange and then successfully pull off "big-deal" activities that might only intimidate both of you.

Let Your Candidate Lead and Teach You

As you get to know the interests, aptitudes, and skills of your candidate, invite her or him to share with you. For example, if the candidate shows an interest in a particular kind of music, admit your own ignorance of it and ask her or him to teach you what makes that music so cool. Be honest in your reactions to it. It's not your opinion or your tastes but your willingness to at least be exposed to what your candidate has to offer that will help solidify the relationship.

If your candidate has a skill you admire, ask her or him to explain its appeal and to teach you the basics of it.

Give Specific Feedback

Young people want and need clear expressions of our interest, affirmation, and support. One way to accomplish this is to avoid generalities ("You're a special person") that they might easily think we would say about anyone.

For example, if your candidate is an active participant in a school event of some kind, make a clear, precise, and affirming comment about that involvement. Instead of saying, "Nice job," say, "That shot you made in the third quarter was great," or "That line you had in act two cracked me up," or "The comment you made to so-and-so while we were leaving was really thoughtful."

The same principle—offering concrete and specific comments rather than general compliments—also applies when you are discussing events at which you are both observers, not active participants. Instead of asking, "What did you think of the play?" (a question that puts a burden on the young person to offer a reasoned opinion on the whole event), say something like: "I really liked the scene when so-and-so did such-and-such. Did any character or scene catch your attention?"

Pray for and with the Candidate

Prayer, both personal and communal, is a central element in Christian spirituality. Make it a point to regularly pray for your candidate. Consider writing a brief, personal daily prayer that you might tape to your mirror as a reminder. Or ask your family to join you in prayer for the candidate at family meals. Try to make a habit of offering a brief, spontaneous prayer in your heart whenever you think of the candidate.

Praying with the candidate presents a greater challenge. Depending on past experiences, this can be awkward for one or both of you. Consider broaching the subject during one of your initial get-togethers; simply ask your candidate how he or she feels about the practice and share your own feelings honestly. Then depending on mutual preferences, consider these options:

- If the particular event or meeting warrants or invites it, consider beginning and ending it with a traditional prayer. For instance, you might start with the Lord's Prayer and end with the Glory Be. Note that the prayers in appendix C of this guide are also found in appendix A of the candidate handbook, making it convenient for you and the candidate to read prayers together.
- Say brief spontaneous prayers related to the events of the day. A natural disaster, an outbreak of violence, the illness of a friend or relative, an upcoming test—virtually anything can prompt a prayer. Consider including a moment during your get-togethers when each of you might offer such prayer intentions.
- If your relationship and comfort level invites it, feel free to offer spontaneous prayer related to the personal concerns and life issues of the candidate. Trust your intuition on this. But also be open to stretching yourself a bit. The experience of shared prayer can be a powerful and potentially life-changing gift to offer the candidate . . . and yourself.

Where and When to Meet

Share What Is Rather Than Create What Isn't

Instead of creating something neat to do together, ask and answer the following questions: (1) Is my candidate already planning to do something I can support by attending or participating? (2) Am I planning to do something that I can invite my candidate to share with me?

Regarding opportunities to involve the candidate in your activities, look for simple, routine things rather than extravaganzas. For example, ask your candidate to help you out with a house or yard project. If you need to make a purchase, ask your candidate for advice and, perhaps, invite her or him to join you while you shop. Obviously, the latter applies most to the purchase of things the candidate has an interest and expertise in—for example, selecting computers, audio or video equipment, music, and so on. Young people, like all of us, need to be needed; when you ask for their help, you affirm their worth.

Program-Related Meetings

Depending on how the Confirmation coordinator chooses to organize the parish's use of Anointed in the Spirit, you may have a number of scheduled opportunities to meet with your candidate. Take full advantage of those connections—meet for a meal before, for a snack afterward, and so on. You may also want to arrange additional get-togethers and take advantage of the step-by-step conversation guide found in the next chapter.

Parish-Sponsored Activities

Every parish calendar includes numerous opportunities to share an event with the candidate, an occasion that connects both of you directly to the life of the broader parish community—a wonderful way to reinforce a major dimension of the Confirmation experience. Possibilities include the following:

- *The regular liturgical life of the parish.* Consider participating together in the Eucharist on a regular basis—maybe on the first weekend of each month.
- *Special seasonal practices, liturgies, and services.* Every liturgical season offers opportunities to share—Advent wreaths, Christmas service projects, stations of the cross, the Easter Vigil, and so on. Be cautious, however, and do not intrude on or otherwise disrupt family traditions—either yours or the candidate's.
- *Special parish events and celebrations.* Most parishes have annual or regularly scheduled events that you might engage in with your

candidate—picnics, patron saint celebrations, project kickoffs, and so on.

- *Opportunities to work together.* Based on the interests and skills of both you and your candidate, volunteer to work together on one or more of the parish's ministries, liturgies, or events.

What to Talk About

Don't Overlook the Obvious

The art of conversation begins with the ability to talk casually about everyday events—including talking about the weather! Keeping in mind your candidate's expressed interests, be alert for any events—school-related, national, almost anything—that you think your candidate might enjoy talking about. And, of course, always invite him or her to suggest topics for conversation.

Share Some "God Talk" . . . with Care

During the early part of the preparation process, you can certainly begin to share with the candidate some conversation about her or his—and your—previous and current faith and religious experience. But do so in ways that are comfortable (nonintrusive and nonthreatening) for both of you.

Having said that, your candidate will expect you to approach her or him about "faith and religion stuff." This is, after all, a Confirmation program. If you appear to avoid the issue, you will send a negative message or give the impression that you are uncomfortable with, or embarrassed by, religious conversation and experience.

One key is to develop the awareness and the skills that allow you to interject and apply faith-centered values, concepts, and insights within and to the situations described above. If you hear a piece of music or see a film or hear a story on the news that invites a faith-centered comment—either pro or con—share it honestly. But always share it as your opinion or insight or value, not as something the young person must embrace to win your respect or friendship.

Another key is to hone your conversation skills. Check out the primer for sponsors on pages 24–30, which offers easy-to-follow principles for fostering significant conversations with young people on faith topics. Then use the guided conversations that follow to move from principles to practice.

An increasing number of young people freely and with genuine conviction embrace Christian faith and value Catholic teachings and practices. Your candidate may expect and be comfortable with conversation about faith and religious practice and even yearn to find an adult who is willing to share such experiences. Even if that's the case, continue to apply all the principles suggested here—listen to the candidate's lived experience, practice one-minute ministry, and so on.

Take Time with the Bible

The sessions in Anointed in the Spirit regularly include the Bible in a variety of ways. The candidate handbook includes short pullout passages from the Scriptures that are related to the session topics. The five guided conversations in the next chapter all incorporate Scripture reading.

An increasing number of young people are attracted to the Bible and interested in exploring its wisdom. Your candidate may be one of them, or he or she may become one of them if you incorporate Scripture reading into your conversations. The Bible may have particular significance for you as well, perhaps even as a central element in your own spiritual life.

Things to Do

Share Your Favorite Catholic Practices

Take some time to reflect on the elements of Catholic life and practice that have particular meaning for you personally, and then consider ways you might share one or more of those elements with your candidate. For example:

- You may have found the stations of the cross to be a valuable spiritual practice. If so, find an opportunity to experience the stations with your candidate, preferably in your own parish church.
- You may read and reflect on the Bible regularly. You could share some of your favorite passages and explain how you reflect on them.
- If you have an ongoing commitment to a particular parish ministry (e.g., religious education, music, service activities), introduce your candidate to that work.

- If the rosary has special significance for you, consider buying one as a special memento for your candidate. Then demonstrate how to say the rosary.
- Consider ways to share with your candidate the importance of the Eucharist in your life.

If applicable, share stories that explain why the practices you choose to share have such meaning for you.

Tour the Candidate's Church

If you tour the candidate's church, you shouldn't presume, of course, that your candidate fully understands the architecture and design of her or his own parish church. Perhaps along with others in the candidate's group, arrange for one of the parish leaders to offer a walking tour of the church, pointing out and providing information about various points of interest—for example, the church's outside architecture, the nave or assembly area, the sanctuary, various examples of religious art, and so on.

Plan a Pilgrimage

The practice of visiting a shrine, a special church (perhaps the diocesan cathedral or a basilica), or a sacred site has a long history in the Catholic Church. Look for opportunities to join with others in such an event (perhaps other candidates and sponsors or the candidate's family might be interested). Be sure the site you visit is recognized and approved by the Church or the local bishop.

Mark or Celebrate Your Candidate's Baptism

During the preparation sessions, the candidates will hear about the strong connection between the Sacraments of Baptism and Confirmation. At some point during the program, each candidate must submit to the parish proof of his or her Baptism, which will include the date it took place. Check with the program coordinator for that information or, if it has not yet been submitted, call your candidate's parent(s) to get the date. Then mark the date of Baptism in a way that seems appropriate—with a card, a meal out, or perhaps a simple gift. For most candidates, this will be the first time the anniversary of their Baptism has been celebrated, raising their awareness of its connection to Confirmation. You might consider a similar practice for the feast day for your candidate's patron saint.

Mark or Celebrate Your Candidate's Confirmation

Based on your shared experience during the process of preparation, consider ways you might mark the event of Confirmation itself. An obvious option is to purchase a gift of some kind, and that is certainly appropriate. If you decide to do that, try to find a gift that truly reflects the nature of the event and will serve as a genuine memento of your time together. A more personal approach might be to write a letter to your candidate expressing your thoughts and feelings as the program draws to a close.

After the Celebration of Confirmation

As mentioned earlier, Anointed in the Spirit includes two sessions designed to take place after Confirmation. These help the newly confirmed reflect on the meaning of Confirmation and consider its significance for their lives and future involvement in the Church.

Find out from the program coordinator how these final two sessions will unfold. Encourage your candidate to take advantage of whatever opportunities for reflection on Confirmation are offered.

In addition consider the ways you might help the young person you sponsored to live out her or his faith in the weeks and months ahead. Possibilities include the following:

- Check in with the candidate after Confirmation, using phone calls or short e-mails.
- Continue doing service projects together.
- Commit to a particular ministry together for a specified period of time.
- Remember special days, such as her or his birthday, important school or extracurricular events, the anniversary of her or his Baptism, and important events for her or his family.
- If you don't complete the five guided conversations in chapter 4 of this guide before Confirmation, continue with them.
- Keep praying for the young person, that she or he will grow closer and closer to God and to the Church.

Chapter 4

Conversations with Young People

A Brief Primer for Sponsors

This section of the guide is intended to help you in your conversations with your candidate. It provides the following information:
- helpful insights about talking with young people
- an outline to help you introduce the conversation process to your candidate (see page 29, "Introducing the Conversation Process at Your First Meeting")
- step-by-step outlines for conversations on the topics of God, Jesus, the Holy Spirit, the Church, and faith

From Barked Commands to Significant Conversations

Young people are a lot like adults. Consider the following similarities:
- They like to talk, but they do not like to be talked at.
- They like to learn, but pretty much only about things that seem relevant to their lives.
- They have hopes and dreams but sometimes need help articulating them.
- They have values but sometimes become disheartened when they can't live up to them.
- They long to love and to be loved, but their emotions are often confusing and they have a hard time expressing them.

Most young people crave healthy conversation with a caring adult, but a significant number are missing this invaluable asset in their lives. For some, their entire day consists of "barked commands": "Get up, get your breakfast, go to school." "Sit down, don't run, get to class." "Do your homework, grab your meal, get to soccer."

At most schools and even churches, too many adults view conversations *between* young people—kids talking to each other—as an interruption, so young people often have to communicate "on the side." For this reason, many young people seem compulsively drawn to text messaging or spending late nights in chat rooms and on social networking Web sites.

In your role as a Confirmation sponsor, you have the opportunity to use an age-old way of learning—one at which our Lord excelled. Jesus' initial words to his first followers (Andrew and John) were not in the form of a lecture or sermon; instead, he sought their input. He asked them a simple and straightforward question: "What are you looking for?" (John 1:38). The Greek verb that Jesus uses in his question *(zateo)* can also be used in the following ways: "What are you *seeking*?" or "What is the *deepest longing* of your life?" Jesus' question to Andrew and John remains one of the *two* most important questions we can ever ask someone whom we hope to guide.

Jesus knew the answer for John and Andrew and was able to present his teaching in a way that was relevant to them. It was so relevant that the first thing they did was run out and tell their family and friends to come meet their new friend, Jesus. Isn't that what we ultimately want? We want to raise young people who are excited and enthusiastic about sharing their faith with those who need hope in darkened situations.

Relevant and Relational Learning

Whenever a subject we are learning does not seem relevant to our lives, our motivation to learn that topic is undermined. It doesn't matter whether it is science, math, geography, values, or religion; we all want to know, "What has this got to do with *my* life?"

It is ultimately the role of the educator to make the topic relevant to the student, not vice versa. Whenever we tie our subject to the candidate's "deepest longing," it becomes relevant.

A great teacher teaches a student—not just a topic. This implies employing a method that is relational, not didactic. It isn't preaching or telling; it is journeying together—sponsor and candidate—using significant conversations. A caring adult can help young people apply what they learn to their lives in ways that enliven faith and help them to embrace meaningful values.

Four Guiding Principles for Conversations

Here are four conversation principles to put into practice when you meet with your candidate:

1. **Introduce the selected topic for conversation, but keep it brief.** Before the meeting, select a topic for your conversation and familiarize yourself with the ideas you want to share. When you meet, introduce the topic to the candidate but get to the conversation as quickly as possible. Aim for a 3:1 ratio. For every 30 minutes you are with your candidate, limit your talking to 10 minutes. Use those 10 minutes to ask questions that will help the young person to verbally explore his or her faith for the other 20 minutes. Spread your 10 minutes throughout the period by asking questions that help the candidate clarify his or her thoughts.

2. **Help your candidate expand her or his vocabulary.** A larger vocabulary has been shown to reduce at-risk behaviors in young people. When young people have the capability to name and discuss emotions with someone they trust, they are better able to think things through before taking action.

    Each conversation in this guide describes some key concepts related to the topic. Try to include these in your conversation and encourage your candidate to put the ideas into her or his own words. This will enable her or him to more readily grasp the concepts, which will give her or him new tools to deal with life.

3. **Encourage storytelling.** A critical part of adolescence is learning how to manage one's emotions and understand the emotional cues of others. The area of the brain responsible for these functions begins to develop during the teenage years. Allowing your candidate to tell stories about experiences related to each topic will deeply increase that topic's impact.

4. **Help your candidate apply the topics of conversation to his or her life.** The concepts we learn do not become a part of our long-term memory until we have either applied them or taught them to someone else. Before your conversation ends, find ways to help your candidate apply what you are discussing or name someone to whom he or she can teach the concepts. This will make faith become a part of his or her lifelong character instead of just being a fact he or she has to remember to be confirmed.

What you are about to offer your candidate can make a lifelong impact on his or her life—his or her eternal life! Please know that God deeply desires to bless you in this endeavor. Enter each conversation with prayer so that the Holy Spirit can assist you in this profoundly vital work.

Conversation Steps

Your candidate will feel more at ease if she or he has a general knowledge of how your sessions will be structured and if you can stick fairly close to that pattern each time you meet. The outlines in this guide follow a three-part pattern:
1. Welcome and introduction of key concepts
2. Scripture reading and conversation
3. Action to deepen the lesson

Tips for "Welcome and Introduction"

Begin each lesson with a brief prayer and by asking about your candidate's week. Try to remember specific events or issues that he or she has shared with you (i.e., an upcoming test or a challenge). Pray with the candidate for God's guidance during your time together and also for those issues that arise during your discussion. Keep this fairly brief.

Spend 3–5 minutes following up on the action steps from the previous week. Share your own experience and ask about the candidate's experience as well.

Give an overview of the current topic and share the key concepts. Remember the 3:1 ratio, keeping this introduction within the time-frame. Allow the candidate to hear the key words and ideas and put them into his or her own language. Multiple studies tell us that expanding a young person's emotional vocabulary reduces his or her at-risk behavior.

Tips for "Scripture Reading and Conversation"

Ask your candidate to read the designated Scripture passage(s) and then begin your discussion. Remember, your key role is to *direct a conversation*, not *lecture about a topic*. As quickly as possible, encourage the young person to begin sharing. It will be harder to start the conversation the first time you are together, but that will change with each progressive meeting as the candidate learns that she or he is safe sharing feelings and ideas with you.

Tips for "Action to Deepen the Lesson"

Move to the action step and agree on taking that action during the week. It may help your candidate to jot some notes that answer the following questions: *What* is the action step? *When* will I take this step? *Where* will I be? *Who* needs to be involved?

After planning the action step, conclude with a prayer of thanksgiving. Share something your candidate did or said that you really appreciated. Be specific. Specific compliments have a lot more power than general statements, plus compliments accent the behaviors you want to encourage. Ask your candidate to tell you what he or she appreciated about your time together as well (learning to praise others is a critical part of a meaningful life). Finally, close with a prayer in which you each thank God for being present in your conversation.

Respectful Learning

You may be wondering, "What is the *other* 'most important question' that we can ask a candidate?" Well, here it is: "How do you want me to treat you?"

> **Three Requests of Young People**
> 1. **Treat me fairly.**
> 2. **Treat me safely.**
> 3. **Be consistent.**

Almost every time I ask young people that question, they say to me, "With respect." When I hear that term, I always ask them, "What does *respect* mean to you?" Over the years, I have heard three distinct responses to that question:

1. Treat me fairly. Don't prejudge me because I am young (or for any other reason).

2. Treat me safely. Let me know by your actions that I will be safe—physically and emotionally—when I am with you.

As a sponsor, this means that not only will you use safe-touch principles with the young person, but you will also shun the use of sarcasm or cynicism when you are with your candidate. Sarcastic humor is almost always at someone else's expense. It is widely used in television today and, sadly, often adults use it to chastise young people. Young people do not have the cognitive ability to grasp sarcasm like the adults around them. Substitute a caring compliment for sarcasm, and you will find the young person much more positive and eager to learn from you.

3. Be consistent. Perhaps the toughest response I hear to the question "What is respect?" is "If you say you are going to show up, then just show up." As sponsors, this means being consistent by following through on our plans.

Introducing the Conversation Process at Your First Meeting

Here are some helpful steps for your first meeting:

1. Welcome your candidate. Start with a simple hello. Ask about your candidate's week. Your candidate needs to know you are interested in her or his life. She or he also needs a general understanding of how the conversation process works. Offer your candidate a simple overview of the format.

2. Ask the candidate to share three ways she or he would like to grow while you study together the next few weeks. Write down those goals, as well as your own. Broad questions like "What would you like to get out of the preparation process for Confirmation?" are difficult for young people to answer. They do better with specific questions like "List three things . . ." Writing will also help the two of you. Use the paper as a reference point rather than having to keep your eyes on each other. It is uncomfortable for some teens to look straight into an adult's eyes. When you have something concrete to view together, you can go back and forth between making eye contact and looking at the paper. Finally, give your candidate

time to respond. If you create the goals, the goals will be yours not hers or his. Keep this list handy so you can occasionally review it.

3. Ask your candidate to create a list of guidelines for how she or he wants to be treated. Have the candidate be specific. For example, if she or he mentions being treated with respect, ask what type of behavior helps her or him feel respected. Add any items you might also consider important, but keep the combined list to a maximum of five items.

Conclusion

Many young people do not have consistent relationships with adults who are not paid to be with them. Our culture can no longer rely on the extended family to assist in the colossal task of raising a child. Young people often live apart from their grandparents and other relatives who used to provide the extra ear or support that both children and parents need at times. As African folk wisdom states, children truly do need a village to raise them.

That's why the work you are doing is so essential. Ultimately, a healthy community is a community in which the adult members know the children among them by name—not just their own children, but other people's children as well. We desperately need parish communities today that focus on this simple but critical characteristic. Our children need communities of intergenerational compassion where adults call them by name, affirming their hopes and dreams.

The LORD says,
"Listen now . . .
I am the LORD who created you;
from the time you were born, I have helped you.
Do not be afraid; you are my servant,
my chosen people whom I love.

(Isaiah 44:1–2, *GNT*)

May God bless you, enrich you, and direct you in this endeavor.

Conversation I
Let's Talk About God

Materials Needed
- a Bible marked at Genesis 1:1–5 and 1 John 4:7–11
- several sheets of paper and two pencils
- two blank index cards

Background Reading for the Sponsor

Young people hear God's name spoken in several contexts. Some may hear it in loving terms during a family meal or prayer. Some may hear it as a swearword used to express anger—maybe at home, in a movie, or in a song. Some hear it spoken at Sunday Mass, and for some this may feel distant from their real life. Some hear God's name spoken reverently by a person or people they admire. This can make a significant impression on young people.

Keep in mind that your candidate chose you as someone he or she admires. He or she will remember far more about the experience you have together than the information you share. You have the opportunity to help this young person recognize God's loving presence in his or her life.

When I talk to young people about God, I keep my conversations as straightforward as possible. Here are two suggested concepts from the Scriptures to talk about with your candidate:

- *God is Creator (see Genesis 1:1–5).* God created the universe with a purpose. We often speak of God creating cosmos (order and purpose) out of chaos (an empty void). God's work of creation continues, and his love and presence never end. God wants us to cooperate with him and to be his coworkers. We are responsible for helping make the world a place where love rules.

- *God is Love (see 1 John 4:7–12).* God loves us without conditions and desires that we love others in the same way. God desires a close relationship with us, our participation in creation, and for us to love others without restrictions.

Conversation Steps

Welcome and Introduction

1. Open with a simple prayer.

2. Ask your candidate about her or his week.

3. Introduce the topic by briefly summarizing the key concepts:
- God is Creator.
- God is Love.

Scripture Reading and Conversation

1. Ask the candidate to read Genesis 1:1–5.

2. Mention that this reading examines the first day of Creation. Explore the concept of creation by asking your candidate how he or she expresses himself or herself creatively. Ask the following questions:
- Do you play music or participate in sports?
- Do you like storytelling, sharing jokes, playing music, or participating in other fine arts?

   Consider discussing the following additional questions:
- Why do people enjoy creative activities?
- What is the difference between being creative and being destructive?
- What does it mean that God is not just creative, but Creator?
- In what ways does God want us to share in creation—as opposed to the destruction—of our world?

3. Work with the candidate to describe ways God is creative.

4. Ask the candidate to read 1 John 4:7–12.

5. Ask the candidate to tell you the difference between true friends who are always there for you and others who only hang around when it benefits them. Take this question a step further and challenge the candidate to come up with three differences between

being loved by someone and being used by someone. Use the paper and pencils to jot down notes.

6. Explain that John tells us that God is the source of love. In other words, he not only loves us but also gives us the strength to love like a true friend. Work with your candidate to identify ways to tap into God's love. Some examples include praying, participating in the Eucharist, providing service to others, and listening to inspiring music. Use the paper and pencils to jot down notes.

Action to Deepen the Lesson

Together with your candidate, create a pocket prayer that will help both of you to remember God's desire to bless your lives. Write out two copies on the blank index cards. Agree to each carry the prayer in your pocket for one week and to say it at least twice a day.

Here's an example:

Dear God, I thank you for this moment. Help me to focus on you. Please help me to remember how much you love me and to have a purpose for my life. Help me to show your love to others and to bring them closer to you as well. Amen.

Conclude by saying the prayer together.

Conversation 2
Let's Talk About Jesus

Materials Needed
- a Bible marked at John 15:12

Background Reading for the Sponsor

Jesus is the Son of God and our Savior. He is fully divine and fully human. He is unlike any other religious leader in history. Aside from his divinity, a number of things make Jesus different from other religious leaders in history. We'll look at three here:

- Jesus didn't emphasize the pursuit of personal fulfillment as much as he emphasized the dignity of all people, especially the most vulnerable. One of his "mission statements," quoted from Isaiah, says that he has come "to bring glad tidings to the poor" (Luke 4:18). To love like Jesus is to empower those whom society often rejects.

- Jesus hung out with sinners. Many religious leaders in Jesus' day not only ignored the diseased and crippled but also avoided sinners as if they were contagious. Jesus sought out sinners and spent time with them. In fact, both the Pharisees and the scribes grumbled about this, saying, "This man welcomes sinners and eats with them" (Luke 15:2).

- Jesus paid special attention to children. Jesus shows us a face of God that children loved. It is one thing for religious leaders to say they love children, but *children loved Jesus.*

To be like Jesus is to seek out the outcasts and to be loved by children. In fact, if we spent our entire lives becoming people that little children loved, we would become an amazing model of the heart of God.

Many religious leaders affirmed the Golden Rule to "love your neighbor as yourself." Jesus goes a step further. Using his own life as a model, he tells his disciples to pay attention to how he loves them and to love others the same way. "This is my commandment: love one another as I love you" (John 15:12).

Conversation Steps

Welcome and Introduction

1. Open with a simple prayer.

2. Ask your candidate about her or his week and follow up on the action step from the previous week.

3. Introduce the key concepts:
- Jesus is unique among religious leaders in human history.
- By word and example, Jesus affirmed the dignity of all people.
- Jesus loves us and calls on us to love others.

Scripture Reading and Conversation

1. Ask the candidate to read John 15:12.

2. Ask the candidate if he or she thinks many young people today believe in a loving God. Then ask if he or she thinks these young people believe that God loves them. Point out that it isn't unusual for teens to believe the former but not the latter. Ask your candidate what his or her views are on why that may be the case.

3. Affirm that Jesus became one of us so we would come to know God's love for us.

4. We know that the consistency of caring adults can help young people come to know God's love. Ask the candidate to identify a person who has been consistent caring in her or his life. See if she or he can name ways the person is like Jesus. Ask her or him to name three qualities of the person.

Action to Deepen the Lesson

Ask the candidate to identify someone he or she would like to be more consistent with. Encourage him or her to name one thing he or she could do to be a more consistent friend to that person. Record the name and the action step.

Conversation 3

Let's Talk About the Holy Spirit

Materials Needed
• a Bible marked at John 14:16–17

Background Reading for the Sponsor

The Holy Spirit is God, one of the three Persons of the Trinity along with the Father and the Son. Help your candidate to learn about the Holy Spirit by introducing some of the Spirit's characteristics.

One characteristic is that the Holy Spirit is an "encourager" and, like a good friend, the Spirit shows up consistently in our lives. The Scriptures refer to the Holy Spirit as "Advocate." Literally, an advocate is someone who would stand up for you in court. "Comforter" is another description of the Holy Spirit. A comforter gives us strength during difficult times.

The presence of the Holy Spirit was evident during the most difficult times of the lives of biblical heroes like Paul, Peter, and the first martyr, Stephen. When religious authorities sought to kill Stephen for testifying about Jesus, the Holy Spirit strengthened the martyr.

The times when our faith is put to the test are the times when we are often most aware of the presence of the Holy Spirit. The Holy Spirit is something like an encouraging coach, but a coach cannot help us improve if we don't show up on the practice field. The practice field of Christianity is wherever we are. This includes the places we routinely find ourselves, but it also includes the places where the lonely need a friend, the forgotten need a smile, or the hungry need a meal. These might be long-term care facilities, homeless shelters, or youth centers that give help to children struggling with school. Some of these practice fields may not be part of your routine or your candidate's routine, but they are probably not too far away. Wherever we are, the Holy Spirit is with us, encouraging us and strengthening us for participation in the Church's mission to help others to know God's love.

Conversation Steps

Welcome and Introduction

1. Open with a simple prayer.

2. Ask your candidate about his or her week and follow up on the action step from the previous week.

3. Introduce the key concepts:
- The Holy Spirit is our Advocate.
- The Holy Spirit encourages us.
- The Holy Spirit comforts us.

Scripture Reading and Conversation

1. Ask the candidate to read John 14:16–17.

2. Talk about the different roles your young person has in her or his life—student, athlete, church member, sister or brother, daughter or son— yet she or he is still one person. Point out to your candidate that all of these roles say something about who she or he is. Explain how we can have a fuller understanding of the Holy Spirit if we understand some of the Holy Spirit's roles or ways of working.

3. Talk about the Holy Spirit as one who encourages us. Ask when your candidate felt encouraged by someone and have him or her elaborate on that experience. What did that person actually do that was encouraging? Ask the candidate what insight this might offer about the Holy Spirit's presence and action in his or her life.

4. Ask, "Has anyone ever stood up for you?" "Have you ever stood up for someone?" Examine the experience to find traits of a person who is an advocate to others. Ask the candidate what insight this might offer about the Holy Spirit's presence and action in her or his life.

5. Share with your young person that the Holy Spirit is also our comforter. Explain that the word *comfort* means "to give strength." Ask about historic figures or people the candidate knows who have given strength to those around them. Ask the candidate what insight this offers about the Holy Spirit's presence and action in his or her life.

Action to Deepen the Lesson

Explain Paul's message to the people of Thessalonia to "encourage one another and build one another up" (1 Thessalonians 5:11). Mention that today we are challenged to cooperate with the work of the Holy Spirit and to encourage one another. Ask the candidate what your parish could do to better encourage young people. Then ask how she or he could contribute to the parish by becoming more encouraging.

Conversation 4
Let's Talk About the Church

Materials Needed
- a Bible marked at Matthew 18:20
- two slips of paper and two pencils

Background Reading for the Sponsor

It is easy to get into the habit of thinking that the Church is a building. However, the original understanding of *church* is rooted in a term meaning "convocation." To *convoke* means "to call together." So, a *convocation* is a group of people who have come together in response to a call. The Church is all the people called together by God. In other words, it isn't just a place you go; it is the person you are, the people you are with, and everyone's connection to God. Jesus elaborates on this concept when he says, "For where two or three are gathered together in my name, there am I in the midst of them" (Matthew 18:20).

Young people today are hungry for a significant faith that will cover many bases: spiritual, personal, social, familial, and meaningful (making a meaningful impact on their world). They are looking for opportunities to be meaningfully engaged in a compassionate community. You help them immensely through your mentoring relationship as a sponsor and by encouraging them to listen to God's call and challenging them to model God's love. You show them an example of what it means to respond to God's call by being present to them with your listening ear and encouraging words. Ultimately, that is what they will look for in a community of faith.

Conversation Steps

Welcome and Introduction

1. Open with a simple prayer.

2. Ask your candidate about his or her week and follow up on the action step from the previous week.

3. Introduce the topic by explaining the key concepts:
- A church is a group of people called together by God.
- It is *who* you are, not just *where* you go.
- Jesus tells us he will be with us when we gather in his name.

Scripture Reading and Conversation

1. Ask the candidate to read Matthew 18:20.

2. Refer to the word *name* that appears in the passage and explain that it also can mean "character." Hebrew names like Jesus had important meanings attached to them. *Jesus* means "Gods saves." Ask your candidate about the character of Jesus. What traits describe him?

3. People often judge us by our character—by what we do, not just what we say. Ask your candidate what it means to gather in Christ's name, if by name we include his character too.

4. Ask your candidate what names or character traits she or he would like other people to use in describing her or him.

Action to Deepen the Lesson

Of the character traits your candidate listed, ask which one he or she would most like people to use in describing him or her. Share your own thoughts as well. Write your candidate's trait and your trait on separate slips of paper and agree to look at your slip every morning and evening. Agree to pray and ask God to help each of you develop these traits. Ask your candidate to try to identify one action related to developing the trait and encourage him or her to do it. Do the same for your trait.

Conversation 5
Let's Talk About Faith

Materials Needed
- two slips of paper and two pencils

Background Reading for the Sponsor

Faith means believing in God, but it means more than that. Faith is the way we respond to God's call in our lives. It guides all of our actions. Growing in faith and deepening our relationship with God takes practice. We can think of faith as a muscle; it gets stronger with exercise and atrophies without it. Help your candidate increase her or his faith by encouraging her or him to tell stories of faithful people she or he knows.

Conversation Steps

Welcome and Introduction

1. Open with a simple prayer.

2. Ask your candidate about his or her week and follow up on the action step from the previous week.

3. Introduce the topic by explaining the key concepts:
- Faith means believing in God and responding to God's call.
- Faith deepens when we practice faithful living.
- Faith is something like a muscle that will atrophy without exercise.

Scripture Reading and Conversation

1. Read, or ask the candidate to read the following passage: "To have faith is to be sure of the things we hope for, to be certain of the things we cannot see" (Hebrews 11:1, *GNT*)

2. Ask your candidate to examine two important words in the passage you read: *sure* and *hope*. If we are "sure" of something, we act with conviction. Ask your candidate about beliefs she or he is sure about. Examples might include "The sun is going to rise" and "Gravity holds us on the earth." Next, ask your candidate some things for which she or he hopes (e.g., "I hope I pass my exams," "I hope to make some new friends," "I hope I have a good day tomorrow"). Work together to identify how a person can turn her or his "hopes" into "sures." Offer this example: "I am more likely to have a good day tomorrow if I help others have a good day too."

3. Ask your candidate to name two or three things he or she hopes for in his or her faith. Offer these examples: eternal life, a close relationship with God, meaningful involvement in a faith community, a way to help others, peacefulness.

4. We become more sure of our hopes if we act on them with conviction. Discuss what habits would help deepen your candidate's assuredness in her or his faith.

Action to Deepen the Lesson

Make a commitment with your candidate to practice at least three actions to strengthen your relationship with God and deepen your faith. Some examples include going to Mass every week, praying every morning, finding concrete actions that help a person in need. Agree to practice these habits for at least four weeks and then contact each other. Share your thoughts about how your faith life has been affected.

This section of the Sponsor Booklet was written by Jerry Goebel. Jerry began his work as an itinerant musician in the early 1970s. After several trips to Central America, Mexico, and the Alaskan wilderness, Jerry decided to focus his ministry on young people who live on the street, who are in gangs, and who are incarcerated. He began Significant Conversations, an outreach program that connects healthy adults with young people in need in order to mentor them in identifying and living by their values. In 2006 Jerry received a lifetime achievement award from the National Federation for Catholic Youth Ministry for living Gospel values.

Appendix A

Central Characteristics of Catholicism

Being Catholic: A Quick View

It is estimated that there are just over one billion Catholics living in the world. That is about 16 percent of the world's population. There are more Catholics than there are people in any other Christian denomination. There are also more Catholics than there are Jews, Hindus, or Buddhists—only Muslims have more members. The great number of Catholics in the world testifies to Catholicism's universal appeal and to the power the Catholic faith has in people's lives.

Here we offer a brief summary of key Catholic beliefs, practices, and attitudes. We do not offer an in-depth explanation as to why Catholics believe or practice what they do. For an in-depth exploration of the Catholic faith, you may wish to purchase *The Catholic Faith Handbook for Youth, Second Edition*, by Brian Singer-Towns (Winona, MN: Saint Mary's Press, 2008), from which the following information about Catholicism has been adapted.

Core Catholic Beliefs

- God created human beings to be in perfect union with God and one another. However, the sin of our first parents—called Original Sin—deprived the human race of our original holiness and justice.
- Throughout human history, God worked to restore the relationship of love and trust that was lost through Original Sin. He did this by entering into covenants—special relationships based on mutual promises—with Noah, Abraham and Sarah, and the people of Israel. But the people often broke their covenant promises.
- Ultimately God sent his only begotten son, Jesus Christ, as savior for the human race. Christ was both fully God and fully man. He

became the perfect sacrifice for the forgiveness of sins and the restoration of the relationship of love and trust between God and humankind.

- Following his death, Jesus was brought back to life in the Resurrection! Christ overcame death and opened Heaven's gates for all the just.
- The Holy Spirit has been at work in the world from the beginning of creation to the present day. The Holy Spirit is one with the Father and the Son and is also called the Advocate (Paraclete) and the Spirit of Truth.
- God has revealed himself to be Trinity, that is, the mystery of one God in three divine Persons: Father, Son, and Holy Spirit. This mystery cannot be arrived at by reason but was revealed by Jesus Christ.
- Christ established the Catholic Church on the foundation of the Apostles. Christ and the Holy Spirit revealed the fullness of religious truth to the Apostles. The fullness of God's revealed truth is called Sacred Tradition and is entrusted to the Apostles' successors, the bishops of the Church.
- The Bible, or the Sacred Scriptures, is another source of God's revealed truth for Catholics. The Bible is closely connected to Sacred Tradition. The Holy Spirit inspired the authors of the Bible to write what God wants us to know for our salvation.
- All people are destined for eternal life after death. The baptized who have put their faith in Jesus Christ as their savior will find their eternal reward in Heaven. Those who have rejected Christ will find their eternal punishment in hell.

Core Catholic Practices

- Catholics celebrate Seven Sacraments that form the basis of their worship, or communal prayer, together. The Seven Sacraments were instituted by Christ and entrusted to the Church to make the love of God real and present in the world.
- The Sacrament of the Eucharist is the heart of the Catholic Church's life. In the sacrament, Catholics literally receive the Body and Blood of Christ in the appearance of bread and wine.

- Sunday, or the "Lord's Day," is the principal day for the celebration of the Eucharist. Catholics keep the day holy by attending Mass and resting from work, in honor of Christ's Resurrection.
- Catholics follow a special calendar with all the feasts and holy days of the liturgical year. The special seasons of Advent and Lent prepare them to understand God's great love, which is celebrated at Christmas and Easter.
- Catholics strongly emphasize living morally because they believe they are called to new life in the Holy Spirit. The moral code for this new life is based on the Ten Commandments and the Beatitudes.
- Catholics defend the dignity of human life, and Catholic morality is often described as pro-life. Catholics are opposed to anything that threatens the sanctity of human life, including abortion, euthanasia, capital punishment, and human cloning.
- Serving people in need and working to transform society are essential elements of Catholic life. The Church is called to be a sign of God's perfect Kingdom yet to come in its fullness, by working for justice and human rights in this life.
- Catholics honor the great people of faith who have preceded them, the saints, and in a dear and special way, Mary, the mother of Jesus.

Core Catholic Attitudes

- Catholics recognize that God is present to, in, and through all creation—including the natural world, persons, communities, and historical events. For Catholics all creation is sacred and has the potential to be a source of God's grace.
- Catholics place their trust in the essential goodness of the human person, who is made in the image of God, even though we are flawed by the effect of Original Sin.
- Catholics appreciate both faith and reason, both religion and science. Reason can lead to faith.
- Although the fullness of truth resides in the Catholic Church, Catholics seek to recognize and affirm the aspects of God's revealed truth that is shared with other religions and all people of goodwill.
- Because the human person is saved by participating in the community of faith—that is, the Church—rather than as an isolated

individual, Catholics emphasize community life and communal worship. Catholics distrust any spirituality that reflects a primary attitude of "it's just God and me; I don't need a Church."

- Catholicism respects the great diversity of cultures in the world and is committed to proclaiming the message of Jesus to all people in all cultures at all times.
- Catholics respect and embrace a wide variety of spiritualities and prayer forms.

Core Catholic Teachings on Reason and Revelation

The Catholic Church makes frequent appeal to human reason in teaching about the religious truths God has revealed. The Church teaches:

- Revelation is God making himself and his Divine Plan known to the human race through words and deeds in human history.
- The human person must trust that God has revealed to the Church what he wants it to know for its salvation.
- In listening to the message of creation and to the voice of conscience, every person can come to certainty about the existence of God.
- Through the natural light of human reason, the one true God can be known from his works—that is, from the world and from the human person. This is one reason why the Church teaches that salvation is possible for every person, even those who have never heard of Jesus Christ.
- God has revealed himself in order to restore the communion that human beings were created to have with him, before the relationship was broken by Original Sin.
- Revelation is communicated in the Bible's stories of how God made himself known to the Chosen People by acting throughout their history. But when those attempts met with failure, God took a radical step. He sent his Son, Jesus Christ, into the world as the Savior. While remaining fully God, Jesus Christ took on a human nature; he is both true God and true man. Thus Jesus Christ is the fullest and complete Revelation of who God is, and through Christ, God established his covenant with the human race forever. As the Bi-

ble tells us, "[Christ] is the image of the invisible God" (Colossians 1:15).

- Everything needed to be known about God and everything needed to be known for eternal union with him has been revealed in Christ. Nothing more needs to be added or taken away.

Core Catholic Teachings on the Scriptures and Tradition

The Catholic Church teaches:

- Christ promised to send the Holy Spirit to his closest followers, the Apostles, after he physically left them to ascend into Heaven: "When he comes, the Spirit of truth, he will guide you to all truth" (John 16:13). The Holy Spirit helped the Apostles to remember and understand all that Jesus did and taught. These truths about Jesus and his teaching are therefore called the Apostolic Tradition, or sometimes just the Tradition.

- Under the inspiration of the Holy Spirit, the Apostles handed on everything they knew about Jesus to the first Christians and to the generation of leaders who followed them.

- The Holy Spirit inspired people in the early Church to create written documents explaining what the Apostles had handed down about Jesus.

- The Scriptures and Tradition are two sources of Revelation. They are closely connected and together form a single sacred deposit of truth under the guidance of the Holy Spirit. They can never be in conflict, and each one helps us to understand the other.

- The Church looks to God's Revelation in the Scriptures and Tradition as the only authentic and complete source for knowledge about God and God's will for the whole human race. It is the responsibility of the Church, through her teaching, her worship, and her ministries, to transmit to every new generation all that God has revealed.

- As the successors of the Apostles, it is the particular and exclusive responsibility of the bishops in union with the Pope—who are also called the Magisterium—to faithfully teach, interpret, and preserve the Scriptures and Tradition for all believers until Christ returns in glory.

The Organization of the Catholic Bible

The books of the Bible are actually organized into sections. The Old Testament has forty-six books divided into the following sections:

- **The Pentateuch (Genesis through Deuteronomy).** These five books are the core of the Old Testament. They tell the stories of Creation, sin, and the origin of God's Chosen People.
- **The Historical Books (Joshua through 2 Maccabees).** These books tell how the Israelites settled in the Promised Land. They also tell the stories of their great—and not-so-great—kings.
- **The Wisdom Books (Job through Sirach).** These are books of poetry and the collected wisdom of the Israelites.
- **The Prophets (Isaiah through Malachi).** These books are the collected speeches and biographies of the Israelite prophets. The prophets spoke for God against idolatry and injustice.

The New Testament has twenty-seven books divided into the following sections:

- **The Gospels (Matthew, Mark, Luke, and John).** These four books are the most important books for Christians because they convey the meaning of Christ Jesus' life and teaching as their central message.
- **The Acts of the Apostles.** This book continues the Gospel of Luke and tells the stories of how the early Church was spread.
- **The Epistles (Romans through Jude).** These are twenty-one letters, written by Paul and other early Church leaders, that give teachings and guidance to individuals and the first Christian churches.
- **The Book of Revelation.** This book records the visions of an early Christian named John.

Core Catholic Understandings on Biblical Inspiration and Interpretation

The way Catholics interpret the Bible has been a source of conflict between Catholics and some other Christians.

- All Christians believe that God is the ultimate author of the Bible because the Holy Spirit inspired the human authors in their writing. But some Christians—sometimes called fundamentalists or literalists—believe that every part of the Bible must be absolutely true in every way: historically true, geographically true, and scientifically true. Thus, for example, they believe that God created the world in six 24-hour days.

- The Catholic Church teaches that the Holy Spirit inspired the biblical authors to write what God wanted known for salvation. The Holy Spirit did not take over the biblical authors' humanity when they wrote. Thus the authors were subject to natural human limitations, and they also used their human creativity in their writing. To continue the earlier example, Catholics believe in the religious truth that God created the world and everything in it, without having to believe that the world was literally created in six 24-hour days.
- Catholics understand that the Bible is without error in communicating what God wants known for salvation without having to be historically and scientifically correct in every detail.

Catholic Beliefs and Practices

This section provides brief summaries of additional Catholic beliefs and practices.

Two Great Commandments

- You shall love the Lord your God with all your heart, with all your soul, with all your mind, and with all your strength.
- You shall love your neighbor as yourself.

(See Matthew 22:37–40, Mark 12:29–31, Luke 10:27.)

Ten Commandments

1. I am the Lord your God: you shall not have strange gods before me.
2. You shall not take the name of the Lord, your God, in vain.
3. Remember to keep holy the Lord's Day.
4. Honor your father and mother.
5. You shall not kill.
6. You shall not commit adultery.
7. You shall not steal.
8. You shall not bear false witness against your neighbor.
9. You shall not covet your neighbor's wife.
10. You shall not covet your neighbor's goods.

Beatitudes (Matthew 5:3–10)

- Blessed are the poor in spirit, for theirs is the kingdom of heaven.
- Blessed are they who mourn, for they will be comforted.
- Blessed are the meek, for they will inherit the land.
- Blessed are they who hunger and thirst for righteousness, for the will be satisfied.
- Blessed are the merciful, for they will be shown mercy.
- Blessed are the clean of heart, for they will see God.
- Blessed are the peacemakers, for they will be called children of God.
- Blessed are they who are persecuted for the sake of righteousness, for theirs is the kingdom of heaven.

Corporal Works of Mercy

- Feed the hungry.
- Give drink to the thirsty.
- Shelter the homeless.
- Clothe the naked.
- Care for the sick.
- Help the imprisoned.
- Bury the dead.

Spiritual Works of Mercy

- Share knowledge.
- Give advice to those who need it.
- Comfort those who suffer.
- Be patient with others.
- Forgive those who hurt you.
- Give correction to those who need it.
- Pray for the living and the dead.

Theological Virtues

- Faith
- Hope
- Love

Cardinal Virtues

- Prudence
- Justice
- Fortitude
- Temperance

Seven Gifts of the Holy Spirit

- **Wisdom.** A wise person recognizes where the Holy Spirit is at work in the world.
- **Understanding.** Understanding helps us to recognize how God wants us to live.
- **Counsel (Right Judgment).** This gift helps us to make choices that will lead us closer to God rather than away from God. The gift of counsel or right judgment helps us to figure out what God wants.
- **Fortitude (Courage).** The gift of fortitude, also called courage, is the special help we need when faced with challenges or struggles.
- **Knowledge.** This gift helps us to understand the meaning of what God has revealed, particularly the Good News of Jesus Christ.
- **Piety (Reverence).** This gift gives us a deep sense of respect for God and the Church. A reverent person honors God and approaches him with humility, trust, and love.
- **Fear of the Lord (Wonder and Awe).** The gift of fear of the Lord makes us aware of God's greatness and power.

Fruits of the Holy Spirit

- Charity
- Joy
- Peace
- Patience
- Kindness
- Goodness
- Generosity (or Long suffering)
- Gentleness (or Humility)
- Faithfulness
- Modesty
- Self-Control (or Continence)
- Chastity

Four Marks of the Catholic Church

- One
- Holy
- Catholic
- Apostolic

Liturgical Year

- Advent
- Christmas
- Ordinary Time
- Lent
- Easter Triduum
- Easter
- Pentecost
- Ordinary Time

Seven Sacraments

- Baptism
- Confirmation
- The Eucharist
- Penance and Reconciliation
- Anointing of the Sick
- Matrimony
- Holy Orders

Precepts of the Church

- Keep holy Sundays and holy days of obligation and attend Mass on these days.
- Confess your sins in the Sacrament of Penance and Reconciliation at least once a year.
- Receive Communion at least during the Easter season.

- Follow the Church's rules concerning fasting and abstaining from eating meat.
- Strengthen and support the Church by providing for the material needs of the Church according to your ability.

Holy Days of Obligation

- Christmas (December 25)
- Solemnity of the Blessed Virgin Mary, the Mother of God (January 1)
- Ascension of the Lord (the Thursday that falls on the fortieth day after Easter, though in some places the celebration is moved to the following Sunday)
- Assumption of the Blessed Virgin Mary (August 15)
- All Saints' (November 1)
- Immaculate Conception of the Blessed Virgin Mary (December 8)

Parts of the Mass

Introductory Rites
- Entrance Chant
- Greeting
- Penitential Act
- *Kyrie*
- Gloria
- Collect (opening prayer)

Liturgy of the Word
- First Reading
- Responsorial Psalm
- Second Reading
- Gospel Acclamation
- Gospel Reading
- Homily
- Profession of Faith
- Prayer of the Faithful

Liturgy of the Eucharist
- Presentation and Preparation of the Gifts
- Prayer over the Offerings

- Eucharistic Prayer
- Communion Rite:
  > Lord's Prayer
  > Sign of Peace
  > Lamb of God
  > Communion
  > Prayer after Communion

Concluding Rites
- Prayer over the People
- Final Blessing
- Dismissal

Appendix B

Overview of the Order of Confirmation

Introductory Rites

The candidates and their sponsors and families, along with other members of the community, gather for the celebration. The candidates may be invited, along with their sponsors, to participate in the opening procession with the bishop, the pastor, and the other liturgical ministers. Everyone stands and sings during the procession.

Liturgy of the Word

All will hear the Word of God proclaimed. The readings are those designated for the day Confirmation is celebrated, or they are specially selected from a list of readings suggested in the *Lectionary*.

Presentation of the Candidates

A leader from the parish presents the candidates to the bishop. Unless the size of the group prevents it, the person making the presentation calls the candidates by name.

Homily

The Liturgy of the Word continues with the homily. The bishop's homily explains the Scripture readings and helps everyone to gain a better understanding of the meaning and significance of the Sacrament of Confirmation.

Renewal of Baptismal Promises

Before the bishop confirms the candidates, he asks them to renew their Baptismal Promises. The Renewal of Baptismal Promises helps to express the close connection between Baptism and Confirmation. The response, a series of "I do's," may appear simple, but the meaning is all important. The candidates are asked to denounce Satan and profess belief in God—Father, Son, and Holy Spirit. The candidates listen to the questions and then loudly and clearly answer, "I do."

The Laying On of Hands

The bishop and the priests lay hands on all the candidates by extending their hands over the whole group. This gesture signifies the gift of the Holy Spirit. The bishop calls on the Father in prayer, asking that he send the Holy Spirit on all the candidates.

The Anointing with Chrism

This is the heart of the Sacrament of Confirmation. Each sponsor places his or her right hand on the shoulder of his or her candidate as a sign of support and commitment to helping the candidate live faithfully. The sponsor presents the candidate to the bishop by telling him the name the candidate has chosen. Then the bishop repeats the candidate's name and anoints him or her. The bishop makes the Sign of the Cross on the candidate's forehead while saying, "Be sealed with the gift of the Holy Spirit." The candidate responds, "Amen," and then exchanges words of peace with the bishop. This is the dialogue between the candidate and the bishop:

Bishop: *(Name),* be sealed with the Gift of the Holy Spirit.

Candidate: Amen.

Bishop: Peace be with you.

Candidate: And with your spirit.

(The Order of Confirmation, 27)

This exchange of peace between the bishop and the candidate is a sign of the bond or close relationship the faithful have with one another and with the bishop.

The General Intercessions

After everyone has been anointed, the community joins together in prayer. Everyone responds, "Lord, hear our prayer," or something similar.

The Liturgy of the Eucharist

When the Sacrament of Confirmation is celebrated within the Mass, which is typical, the celebration continues with the Liturgy of the Eucharist. This helps to highlight the unity of the three Sacraments of Initiation and the communion among all the people with God. At the end of the Mass, everyone is sent forth to love and serve the Lord.

Appendix C
Catholic Prayers

Act of Contrition

My God, I am sorry for my sins
with all my heart, and I detest them.
In choosing to do wrong and failing to do good,
I have sinned against you,
whom I should love above all things.
I firmly intend, with your help,
to do penance, to sin no more,
and to avoid whatever leads me to sin.
Our savior Jesus Christ suffered and died for us.
In his name, my God, have mercy.

Act of Faith

My God, I firmly believe you are one God in three Divine Persons,
Father, Son, and Holy Spirit.
I believe in Jesus Christ, your Son, who became man and died for our
sins, and who will come to judge the living and the dead.
I believe these and all the truths which the Holy Catholic Church
teaches, because you have revealed them, who can neither deceive
nor be deceived.
Amen.

Act of Hope

O my God, trusting in your infinite goodness and promises, I hope to
obtain pardon of my sins, the help of your grace, and life everlasting,
through the merits of Jesus Christ, my Lord and redeemer. Amen.

Act of Love

My God, I love you above all things, with my whole heart and soul, because you are all-good and worthy of all my love. I love my neighbor as myself for love of you. I forgive all who have injured me, and I ask pardon of all whom I have injured. Amen.

Angelus

The angel of the Lord declared unto Mary,
And she conceived of the Holy Spirit.
　　Hail Mary . . .
Behold the handmaid of the Lord,
Be it done unto me according to your word.
　　Hail Mary . . .
And the Word was made flesh,
And dwelt among us.
　　Hail Mary . . .
Pray for us, O Holy Mother of God, that we may be made worthy of the promises of Christ. Let us pray: Pour forth, we beseech you, O Lord, your grace into our hearts that we to whom the incarnation of Christ, your Son, was made known by the message of the angel may, by his passion and cross, be brought to the glory of his resurrection, through Christ our Lord.

Apostles' Creed

I believe in God, the Father almighty,
Creator of heaven and earth, and in Jesus Christ, his only Son, our Lord, who was conceived by the Holy Spirit, born of the Virgin Mary, suffered under Pontius Pilate, was crucified, died and was buried; he descended into hell; on the third day he rose again from the dead; he ascended into heaven, and is seated at the right hand of God the Father almighty; from there he will come to judge the living and the dead.

I believe in the Holy Spirit, the holy catholic Church, the communion of saints, the forgiveness of sins, the resurrection of the body, and life everlasting. Amen.

Blessing of Chrism

God our maker,
source of all growth in holiness,
accept the joyful thanks and praise
we offer in the name of your Church.

In the beginning, at your command,
the earth produced fruit-bearing trees.
From the fruit of the olive tree
you have provided us with oil for holy chrism.
The prophet David sang of the life and joy
that the oil would bring us in the sacraments of your
    love.

After the avenging flood,
the dove returning to Noah with an olive branch
announced your gift of peace.
This was a sign of a greater gift to come.
Now the waters of baptism wash away the sins of
    men,
and by the anointing with olive oil
you make us radiant with your joy.

At your command,
Aaron was washed with water,
and our servant Moses, his brother,
anointed him priest.
This too foreshadowed greater things to come.
After your Son, Jesus Christ our Lord,
asked John for baptism in the waters of Jordan,
you sent the Spirit upon him
in the form of a dove
and by the witness of your own voice
you declared him to be your only, well-beloved Son.
In this you clearly fulfilled the prophecy of David,
that Christ would be anointed with the oil of gladness
beyond his fellow men.

And so, Father, we ask you to bless this oil you
    have created.

Fill it with the power of your Holy Spirit
through Christ your Son.
It is from him that chrism takes its name
and with chrism you have anointed
for yourself priests and kings,
prophets and martyrs.

Make this chrism a sign of life and salvation
for those who are to be born again in the waters of
     baptism.
Wash away the evil they have inherited from sinful
     Adam,
And when they are anointed with this holy oil
make them temples of your glory,
radiant with the goodness of life
that has its source in you.

Through this sign of chrism
Grant them royal, priestly, and prophetic honor,
and clothe them with incorruption.
Let this be indeed the chrism of salvation
for those who will be born again of water and the
     Holy Spirit.
May they come to share eternal life
in the glory of your kingdom.
We ask this through Christ our Lord.
Amen.

Confiteor (I Confess)

I confess to almighty God and to you, my brothers and sisters, that I
have greatly sinned in my thoughts and in my words, in what I have
done and in what I have failed to do, through my fault, through my
fault, through my most grievous fault; therefore I ask blessed Mary
ever-Virgin, all the Angels and Saints, and you, my brothers and sisters, to pray for me to the Lord our God.

Glory Be

Glory be to the Father, and to the Son, and to the Holy Spirit, as it
was in the beginning, is now, and will be forever. Amen.

Grace Before Meals

Bless us, O Lord, and these your gifts,
which we are about to receive
from your bounty,
through Christ our Lord. Amen.

Grace After Meals

We give you thanks, almighty God,
for these and all your gifts
which we have received
through Christ our Lord. Amen.

Hail Mary

Hail Mary, full of grace,
the Lord is with you;
blessed are you among women,
and blessed is the fruit of your womb, Jesus.

Holy Mary, Mother of God,
pray for us sinners
now and at the hour of our death.
Amen.

Lord's Prayer (Our Father)

Our Father who art in Heaven,
hallowed be thy name.
Thy kingdom come.
Thy will be done on earth, as it is in Heaven.
Give us this day our daily bread,
and forgive us our trespasses,
    as we forgive those who trespass against us,
and lead us not into temptation,
but deliver us from evil. Amen.

Magnificat (Mary's Song) (See Luke 1:46–55)

My being proclaims the greatness of the Lord,
my spirit finds joy in God my savior.

For he has looked upon his servant
in all her lowliness.
All ages to come shall call me blessed.
God who is mighty
has done great things for me, holy is his name;
his mercy is from age to age
on those who fear him.
He has shown might with his arm;
he has confused the proud
in their inmost thoughts.
He has deposed the mighty from their thrones
and raised the lowly to high places.
The hungry he has given every good thing
while the rich he has sent empty away.
He has upheld Israel his servant,
ever mindful of his mercy,
even as he promised our fathers,
promised Abraham and his descendants
forever.

Memorare

Remember, O most gracious Virgin Mary, that never was it known that anyone who fled to your protection, implored your help, or sought your intercession was left unaided. Inspired by this confidence, we fly unto you, O virgin of virgins, our mother. To you do we come, before you we stand, sinful and sorrowful. O mother of the Word Incarnate, despise not our petitions, but in your mercy, hear and answer us.

Morning Prayer

Almighty God, I thank you for your past blessings. Today I offer myself—whatever I do, say, or think—to your loving care. Continue to bless me, Lord. I make this morning offering in union with the divine intentions of Jesus Christ who offers himself daily in the holy sacrifice of the Mass, and in union with Mary, his Virgin Mother and our Mother, who was always the faithful handmaid of the Lord. Amen.

Nicene Creed

I believe in one God, the Father almighty, maker of heaven and earth, of all things visible and invisible.

I believe in one Lord Jesus Christ, the Only Begotten Son of God, born of the Father before all ages. God from God, Light from Light, true God from true God, begotten, not made, consubstantial with the Father; through him all things were made. For us men and for our salvation he came down from heaven, and by the Holy Spirit was incarnate of the Virgin Mary, and became man.

For our sake he was crucified under Pontius Pilate, he suffered death and was buried, and rose again on the third day in accordance with the Scriptures. He ascended into heaven and is seated at the right hand of the Father. He will come again in glory to judge the living and the dead and his kingdom will have no end.

I believe in the Holy Spirit, the Lord, the giver of life, who proceeds from the Father and the Son, who with the Father and the Son is adored and glorified, who has spoken through the prophets.

I believe in one, holy, catholic and apostolic Church. I confess one Baptism for the forgiveness of sins and I look forward to the resurrection of the dead and the life of the world to come. Amen.

Prayer of Saint Francis

Lord, make me an instrument of your peace:
    where there is hatred, let me sow love;
    where there is injury, pardon;
    where there is doubt, faith;
    where there is despair, hope;
    where there is darkness, light;
    where there is sadness, joy.
Divine Master,
    grant that I may not so much seek
    to be consoled as to console,
    to be understood as to understand,

to be loved as to love.
For it is in giving that we receive,
  it is in pardoning that we are pardoned,
  it is in dying that we are born to eternal life.

Prayer to the Holy Spirit

Come, Holy Spirit, fill the hearts of your faithful. Enkindle in them the fire of your love. Send forth your Spirit, and they will be created. And you will renew the face of the earth.
Let us pray:
Lord, by the light of the Holy Spirit, you have taught the hearts of the faithful. In the same Spirit, help us to relish what is right and always rejoice in your consolation. We ask this through Christ our Lord. Amen.

Renewal of Baptismal Promises (*The Order of Confirmation,* 23)

Bishop: Do you renounce Satan and all his works and empty promises?
Candidates: I do.
Bishop: Do you believe in God, the Father almighty, Creator of heaven and earth?
Candidates: I do.
Bishop: Do you believe in Jesus Christ, his only Son, our Lord, who was born of the Virgin Mary, suffered death and was buried, rose again from the dead and is seated at the right hand of the Father?
Candidates: I do.
Bishop: Do you believe in the Holy Spirit, the Lord, the giver of life, who today through the Sacrament of Confirmation is given to you in a special way just as he was given to the Apostles on the day of Pentecost?
Candidates: I do.
Bishop: Do you believe in the holy Catholic Church, the communion of saints, the forgiveness of sins, the resurrection of the body, and life everlasting?
Candidates: I do.

Rosary

The Rosary is perhaps the most popular devotion to Mary, the Mother of God. The central part of the Rosary consists of the recitation of five sets of ten Hail Marys (each set is called a decade). Each new decade begins by saying an Our Father, and each decade concludes with a Glory Be. Individuals keep track of the prayers said by moving from one bead to the next in order.

The recitation of the Rosary begins with a series of prayers, said in the following order while using as a guide a small chain of beads and a crucifix:

1. the Sign of the Cross
2. the Apostles' Creed
3. one Our Father
4. three Hail Marys
5. one Glory Be

After these introductory prayers, the recitation of the decades begins.

The saying of a five-decade Rosary is connected with meditation on what are called the mysteries of the life of Jesus. These mysteries too are collected into series of five—five joyful, five luminous, five sorrowful, and five glorious mysteries. Individuals who are praying devote one recitation of the Rosary to each set of mysteries. They choose which set of mysteries to meditate on while saying the decades of Hail Marys. Therefore, the *complete* Rosary consists of twenty decades.

With a little practice, the regular praying of the Rosary can become a source of great inspiration and consolation for Christians.

Joyful Mysteries
- The Annunciation
- The Visitation
- The Birth of Our Lord
- The Presentation of Jesus in the Temple
- The Finding of Jesus in the Temple

Luminous Mysteries
- The Baptism of Jesus
- Jesus Reveals Himself in the Miracle at Cana
- Jesus Proclaims the Good News of the Kingdom of God
- The Transfiguration of Jesus
- The Institution of the Eucharist

Sorrowful Mysteries
- The Agony of Jesus in the Garden
- The Scourging at the Pillar
- The Crowning of Thorns
- The Carrying of the Cross
- The Crucifixion

Glorious Mysteries
- The Resurrection of Jesus
- The Ascension of Jesus into Heaven
- The Descent of the Holy Spirit on the Apostles (Pentecost)
- The Assumption of Mary into Heaven
- The Crowning of Mary as Queen of Heaven

Sign of the Cross

In the name of the Father, and of the Son, and of the Holy Spirit. Amen.

Stations of the Cross

1. Jesus is condemned to death.
2. Jesus takes up his cross.
3. Jesus falls the first time.
4. Jesus meets his mother.
5. Simon helps Jesus carry the cross.
6. Veronica wipes the face of Jesus.
7. Jesus falls the second time.
8. Jesus meets the women of Jerusalem.
9. Jesus falls the third time.
10. Jesus is stripped of his garments.
11. Jesus is nailed to the cross.
12. Jesus dies on the cross.
13. Jesus is taken down from the cross.
14. Jesus is laid in the tomb.

Acknowledgments

Scriptural quotations in this publication labeled *GNT* are from the *Good News Translation*® (Today's English Version, Second Edition). Copyright © 1992 by the American Bible Society. All rights reserved. Bible text from the *Good News Translation (GNT)* is not to be reproduced in copies or otherwise by any means except as permitted in writing by the American Bible Society, 1865 Broadway, New York, NY 10023 *(www.americanbible.org)*.

All other scriptural quotations in this book are from the *New American Bible with Revised New Testament and Revised Psalms (NAB)*. Copyright © 1991, 1986, and 1970 by the Confraternity of Christian Doctrine, Washington, D.C. Used by the permission of the copyright owner. All rights reserved. No part of the New American Bible may be reproduced in any form without permission in writing from the copyright owner.

The prayers, devotions, beliefs, and practices contained herein have been verified against authoritative sources.

The excerpts on pages 6, 58, 67, and the back cover are from the English translation of *The Order of Confirmation* © 2013, International Commission on English in the Liturgy Corporation (ICEL), 33, 27, 27, 23, and 22, respectively. All rights reserved. Used with permission. Texts contained in this work derived whole or in part from liturgical texts copyrighted by ICEL have been published here with the confirmation of the Committee on Divine Worship, United States Conference of Catholic Bishops. No other texts in this work have been formally reviewed or approved by the United States Conference of Catholic Bishops.

The information in chapters 2 and 3 is adapted from *Confirmed in a Faithful Community: A Senior High Confirmation Process: Sponsor's Guide,* Third Edition (Winona, MN: Saint Mary's Press, 2006). Copyright © 2006 by Saint Mary's Press. All rights reserved.

The excerpt on page 10 is from the English translation, original text, additional notes and arrangement of *Rite of Christian Initiation of Adults* © 1985 ICEL, in *The Rites of the Catholic Church*, volume one, prepared by the ICEL, a Joint Commission of Catholic